PROZAC:
THE CONTROVERSIAL CURE

Prozac is a drug given to people who are diagnosed with depression.

PROZAC:
THE CONTROVERSIAL CURE

Helen C. Packard

THE ROSEN PUBLISHING GROUP, INC.
NEW YORK

for Emily

The people pictured in this book are only models. They in no way practice or endorse the activities illustrated. Captions serve only to explain the subjects of photographs and do not in any way imply a connection between the real-life models and the staged situations.

Published in 1998 by The Rosen Publishing Group, Inc.
29 East 21st Street, New York, NY 10010

Copyright © 1998 by The Rosen Publishing Group, Inc.

Library of Congress Cataloging-in-Publication Data

Packard, Helen C.
  Prozac : the controversial cure / Helen C. Packard
  p.   cm.   — (Drug abuse prevention library)
  Includes bibliographical references and index.
  Summary: Discusses the drug Prozac and its use in treatment of depression.
    ISBN 0-8239-2551-X
    1. Fluoxetine—Juvenile literature.
    2. Depression, Mental—Juvenile literature.
    [1. Fluoxetine.   2. Depression, Mental.]
    I. Title.   II. Series.
    RC483.5.F55P33   1997
    616.85′27061—dc21   97-44529
                                                   CIP
                                                    AC

Manufactured in the United States of America

Contents

Introduction

Audrey just couldn't shake her bad mood. She often felt blue or down and had trouble getting out of bed in the morning. She was always tired, even when she got enough sleep at night. The smallest tasks, like brushing her teeth or making her bed, became a huge effort.

Audrey used to hang out with her friends every day after school, but lately she has gone straight home and crawled back into bed. Sometimes she hid food under her bed. Eating made Audrey feel better for a little while and helped her forget how lonely she had been since her parents' divorce. But there was always an ache somewhere above her stomach that never went away.

After about a month, Audrey's mom realized

that this was more than a bad mood and took her to the family doctor. The doctor asked Audrey some questions about her feelings, and Audrey tried to explain. She didn't understand why she felt so down all the time, and it made her angry and frustrated. But at the same time, she just didn't care about anything.

The doctor listened very carefully to what Audrey said. He asked if there had been any difficult situations in the family recently, or if Audrey or her mother knew of anyone in the family who had ever been depressed. Audrey's mother mentioned her divorce and recalled that she herself had been depressed when she was a teenager.

The doctor told Audrey that she was suffering from depression. He gave her the name of a therapist to visit on a regular basis to talk about her feelings. He also prescribed a medication called Prozac.

Have you ever felt like Audrey? If you have, you're not alone. Millions of Americans suffer from a condition called depression. Depression is not just a few days of feeling down in the dumps because your team lost the state softball championships, or a weekend of feeling sad because your new crush in history class hasn't called.

8 | Depression is a psychological disorder marked by extreme sadness, inactivity, difficulty in concentrating, increased or decreased appetite, sleep disturbances, feelings of hopelessness, and sometimes suicidal tendencies. When it's particularly severe, the disorder is known as clinical depression.

Some people who feel depressed talk to a therapist or a psychiatrist about their problems. But some people find they need more help. That's when many people are given a medication. Prozac is one of these medications. It has been called the "wonder drug," or the "miracle drug." Many people have found that it helps to relieve their depression or other problems. Some people have even given it to their pets!

But although many people have benefited from Prozac, problems have also developed. Some depressed people report having violent mood swings or even thoughts of hurting themselves or others while taking Prozac. Some say Prozac is prescribed too often and under the wrong conditions. This can be very dangerous. It can even make the depression worse by creating other physical and psychological reactions.

This book talks about what Prozac is, why someone might take it, and what to look for if you think you're experiencing depression. It also talks about warning signs that Prozac may be harming instead of helping you, and about the controversy and dangers surrounding Prozac today.

Being depressed and taking medication like Prozac does not mean you're "crazy." It means you're recognizing your feelings and doing something positive about your situation. Taking care of yourself is a good choice. But it's important for your own health to know all the facts.

You may feel sad, upset, angry, and frustrated and not know why. These are symptoms of depression.

CHAPTER 1

What Is Prozac?

Emily didn't get it. She sat on her bed and thought about it some more. School was going okay. She was getting her work done, although she wasn't interested in her favorite classes anymore. She used to look forward to geometry, and she had even gotten the hang of French class. But lately, Emily had no interest in her favorite class—or in anything, for that matter. She was even too tired to go to karate on Wednesdays, and that was something she had never missed.

Even though Emily was exhausted all day, when she went to bed she lay awake all night long, tossing and turning. Her clothes were getting too big for her, because she was never hungry. Emily looked around her room, feeling more and more frustrated and down. It made

12 | *her angry, but at the same time she didn't really care. She just wanted to curl up, stare at the wall, and fall asleep forever. Why was she so out of it? What was going on?*

Everyone has felt depressed at one time or another. Feeling down is one kind of response when sad or difficult things happen. But sometimes a person can feel down or blue for a long time, perhaps a month or more, and it affects his daily life. That person may be suffering from depression. He or she may have some of the following symptoms:

- Feelings of sadness most or all of the time
- Lack of energy or a loss of interest in activities
- Difficulty in concentrating
- Trouble sleeping
- Eating too much or too little
- Frequent stomachaches or headaches
- Feelings of guilt, worthlessness, or ugliness
- Suicidal thoughts

Any or all of these symptoms can be very frightening, especially when a person does not understand what is happening.

Difficult or stressful situations may contribute to the onset of depression.

Causes of Depression

Teenagers are especially susceptible to depression. This may be, in part, because of the change from adolescence to adulthood. Many physical and emotional changes occur during this time, and it can be frustrating and scary. As a teenager, you may not understand why you are experiencing bodily changes or different feelings, and this can make you feel scared, anxious, or depressed.

Scientists believe there are several causes of depression. Some think depression is caused by a crisis, such as the death of a loved one, family problems, or other big changes in a person's life, such as adolescence. Other scientists believe

14 | that depression is hereditary. That means that if someone in your family has suffered from depression, you are more likely to suffer from it.

Another theory is that depression comes from loss. A loss does not have to be something one can see or hear; it can also be something inside oneself, such as self-esteem, confidence, or hope. Still another belief is that depression comes from chemical changes in the brain.

Depression could also result from a combination of any or all of these causes.

Treating Depression

Depression can be very serious, or even fatal, if it is not treated. Fortunately, help is available in different forms. Some people go to their doctor or a therapist for help when depression starts to take over their lives.

A family doctor or therapist may first recommend a few steps before deciding on medication.

Alternatives to Medication

- **Change in diet:** Your doctor may suggest that you eat more fruits and vegetables and cut down on processed or sugary foods.

Exercising and eating healthy foods are good ways to deal with your depression.

16

- **A regular exercise program:**
  Exercising three to four times a
  week, thirty to forty minutes at a
  time. This can stimulate chemicals in
  the brain called endorphins that act
  as natural antidepressants and can
  lift a person's mood.
- **Therapy:** Weekly or biweekly visits
  to a therapist to talk about your
  feelings.

What if a depressed person has talked
with the doctor and has tried a healthier
diet, regular exercise, *and* therapy, but
still feels down most or all of the time?
That's when antidepressants come into
the picture.

Antidepressants

An antidepressant is a drug that relieves
depression or another condition related to
the depression. The antidepressant affects
chemicals in the brain, which can be
either working too hard or not working
hard enough, depending on the kind of
depression the person has.

There are several kinds of antidepressants for different kinds of depression.
One kind of depression makes a person
feel tired all the time, and he or she often

overeats. In another form of depression, a person may not be able to sleep and has no appetite.

If you are experiencing any of the symptoms mentioned earlier, your doctor may recommend that you see another doctor, such as a psychiatrist. A psychiatrist is a therapist, but he or she is also a medical doctor and can write prescriptions for medications. Your family doctor may also write you a prescription for an antidepressant and suggest that you visit a therapist.

Julio used to love history class. But lately, he hasn't been able to get excited about history or anything else. Mr. Walker, the history teacher, noticed that Julio hadn't been paying attention in the past few weeks. Julio also asked to be excused from class twice last week because he didn't feel well.

When Mr. Walker asked him about it, Julio said he didn't know what was wrong—he just felt sad and tired most of the time. Mr. Walker was worried about his student and called Julio's parents.

Julio's parents took him to a psychiatrist. The doctor talked with Julio and his parents. He recommended a therapist whom Julio could see regularly, and then prescribed Prozac for Julio.

18 | ## *Prozac*

Prozac is an antidepressant. It has become the most popular and best-selling antidepressant in the United States. Prozac has been prescribed for 21 million people, and sales of the drug reached $350 million just one year after its introduction in 1988. By 1990, 650,000 prescriptions for Prozac were being written each month. In 1995, sales of the drug reached $2 billion. Today, Prozac adds to the 1.3 million prescriptions written annually for antidepressants. The most common use for Prozac is in cases of clinical depression.

Prozac, also known by its scientific name fluoxetine, belongs to a new group of antidepressants called selective serotonin reuptake inhibitors, or SSRIs, that have been created in the past decade. Before Prozac and its family of antidepressants were introduced, doctors prescribed other antidepressants. But they were slow to take effect, caused severe side effects, and often made people feel "zonked" or "out of it." In some major cases of depression, electroconvulsive therapy, or shock treatments, were performed. They are still used today with much success.

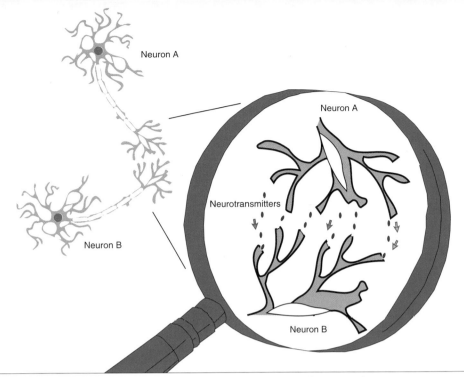

Neuron A

Neuron A

Neurotransmitters

Neuron B

Neuron B

Antidepressants work in synapses, the spaces between brain cells.

But with the introduction of Prozac and its family of medications, patients did not have to wait up to a month for a medication to take effect, did not have to experience unpleasant side effects, and often did not feel "out of it." These antidepressants work deep inside the brain, in the spaces between brain cells called synapses. In the synapses, a chemical called serotonin acts as a messenger for the brain. Serotonin carries messages across synapses from brain cell to brain cell, to the rest of the body.

For some people, serotonin is not a very good messenger. It may not stay in the synapse long enough to carry messages, or it may be stolen back by the

19

Alcohol can cause a dangerous reaction when mixed with antidepressants.

first brain cell and not carry any message
at all. Prozac and its related antidepressants help to keep serotonin in the
synapse longer, so the brain can send its
messages all over the body. Researchers
believe that this helps depressed people
feel less depressed.

However, everyone's body is different.
Like any other medicine, Prozac may
work well for one person and not work
well for another. If you and your doctor
decide that Prozac or another antidepressant might help you, make sure your
doctor is aware of *all* other medications
that you are taking. Even something as
simple as an over-the-counter cold medicine can produce a harmful reaction
when used with some antidepressants.

And most important, do not mix
alcohol or any illegal drug with Prozac or
other antidepressants. Any of these com-
binations could make you very sick. They
could even be life-threatening.

*Joey was excited. He had been looking
forward to Hannah's party for weeks. Since
he started taking Prozac last month, Joey
had felt much better.*

*There were already a lot of people in
Hannah's basement when Joey arrived. The*

22 *music was loud, and it was hot and crowded, but Joey was glad to be going out again. He saw his friends, Jay and Toni, in the corner. He grabbed a soda from the table and went over to them.*

"Joey! What's up?" Toni slurred her words as she gave Joey a huge, sloppy hug.

"Joey, man, you want me to freshen that drink for you?" Jay asked, showing a bottle of liquor hidden behind his back.

Joey felt caught. When he started Prozac, his doctor had told him that he shouldn't have any alcohol. Alcohol could cause a dangerous reaction with the antidepressant. Joey didn't want to sound like a wimp to his friends, but he knew that alcohol and antidepressants don't mix. "Uh, no thanks, man. I'm just not into it tonight. Hey, what's up with this music?"

"I know, it sucks!" Toni said. "Let's pick out another CD. Hannah has plenty over there." She put down her cup.

"No drink, Joey? What's the problem?" Jay asked.

"Leave him alone, Jay," Toni said. "If he's not into it, he's not into it. Come on, Joey."

"Hey, it's cool, man," Jay said, giving Joey a light slap on the back. "Go find some real music over there, guys. I'll wait here."

"You got it," Joey smiled.

How Long Do People Take Prozac?

The length of time a person takes Prozac or another antidepressant depends on the depression or other condition with which the person is afflicted. If the depression is caused by a crisis or situation that comes to an end, or if the depression is handled through therapy and an antidepressant, the person may be on Prozac for only six months or so. If the person has a chronic depression, or one that returns because of a chemical imbalance in the brain, a series of crises, or a combination of both, Prozac may be taken longer.

Prozac Is Popular

More than 6 million people in the United States and an additional 4 million people around the world have taken Prozac. Many people have had positive experiences with the drug. It is popular for many reasons:

- It has fewer side effects than other antidepressants.
- It takes only two to four weeks to work, whereas other antidepressants can take at least six weeks to show results.
- Many patients need to take only one

24

pill daily, as opposed to other medications, where more are sometimes necessary.

- It is often highly effective.

Prozac has become a very popular antidepressant with teenagers, because of its fewer side effects and its faster response time.

But Prozac does have some side effects. Not all people who take Prozac experience these side effects, and the effects often disappear after a few weeks. They include:

- Insomnia (trouble falling asleep at night or waking up often during the night)
- Nausea, diarrhea, or stomach cramps
- Nervousness
- Headache
- Drowsiness

CHAPTER 2

What Else Does Prozac Treat?

*A*lthough Prozac has been used mostly to treat depression, it is currently being used more and more. It has been shown to work for a variety of disorders, although scientists cannot always explain why. This chapter explores some of those conditions.

Obsessive-Compulsive Disorder

Obsessive-compulsive disorder, or OCD, affects as many as one in 100 people. A person with OCD feels a strong but irrational need to repeat certain behaviors, such as washing one's hands or checking that the stove has been turned off. Imagine feeling that you must wash your hands four or five times in two hours, or

26 | checking your homework fifty times for fear you missed a math problem. The person with OCD is obsessed with repetitive behavior. If he does not do the repetitive behavior, he is overcome by an anxiety so severe that he cannot function. He can think of nothing but completing the repetitive behavior. Prozac has often been prescribed for people with OCD, with positive results.

Phobias

People who suffer from phobias are also being given Prozac. Phobias are extreme fears about things or situations. For example, acrophobia is the fear of heights, and claustrophobia is a fear of small spaces. Many people are afflicted with these fears. But the fear is considered a phobia only if it interferes with one's daily life.

Other Conditions

Prozac is being prescribed for people who are subject to migraine, a condition in which severe headaches occur, often accompanied by nausea and vomiting. Scientists have found that the raised serotonin levels in the brain produced by Prozac sometimes help people with migraine.

Prozac sometimes is prescribed for people who suffer from migraine headaches.

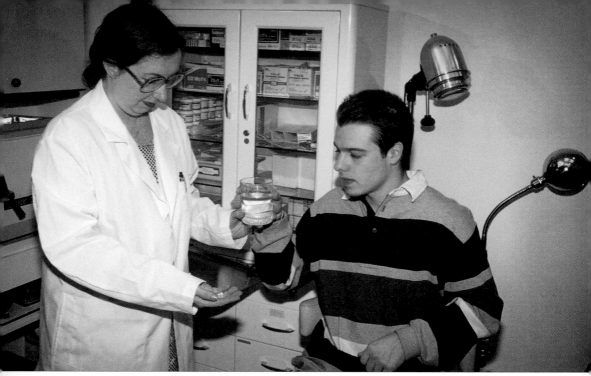

More and more teens are relying on Prozac for a growing number of reasons.

Premenstrual syndrome, or PMS, is another condition for which Prozac is being used. PMS occurs in menstruating females before a menstrual period begins. This time is full of hormonal changes, which can cause depression, anxiety, irritability, headaches, and cramps. Prozac helps to lessen some of these problems.

Prozac also has been prescribed for certain eating disorders.

Marie first noticed something was wrong when she went to the movies with her friends. She looked at the people sitting around her and felt trapped. Fear seemed to take her over, and she had trouble breathing or focusing on the movie screen.

A few days later Marie's fear worsened. Even a trip to the supermarket made it hard for her to breathe, and she felt as if everyone was watching her. She was afraid at school, at church, and at her friends' houses. Whenever she left home, she had trouble breathing and began to sweat. She didn't understand what was happening to her.

Marie went to a psychiatrist and talked about fear when she tried to leave the house. The doctor decided that she was suffering from a condition called agoraphobia. Marie started taking Prozac.

After about three weeks, Marie no longer had trouble breathing when she arrived at school in the morning, and she didn't feel that everyone was watching her.

About 8 million of the 53 million American teenagers today suffer from some emotional or mental disorder, including depression and many of the other disorders just described. Prozac has become a common name in homes and schools across the nation.

Miko looked at the school clock as the bell rang for fifth period. 12:15—time for her medicine. Miko shoved her books into her bookbag and followed the other students

30 | *toward the cafeteria. But instead of taking a right into the lunchroom, Miko continued down the hall to the nurse's office. Mrs. Spar, the school nurse, had a special cabinet where all of the students' medications were kept. Miko's Prozac was in that cabinet.*

Miko walked into Mrs. Spar's office. Five or six other students were waiting at the nurse's desk while she unlocked the cabinet. Miko recognized a girl from her gym class, and smiled. The girl smiled back.

Miko noticed that some of the other kids were taking Prozac, too. She had always been embarrassed about coming to the nurse's office for her medicine every day. But now it seemed like part of the routine.

Even more important, Prozac was helping Miko's depression. She had been taking it for about eight weeks, and the weight that had been pushing on her shoulders was lifting. Miko was feeling better.

"Here you go, Miko," Mrs. Spar said. She handed Miko a pill and a paper cup. Miko swallowed her medicine with water from the water fountain and said good-bye to Mrs. Spar.

Some people benefit from taking Prozac for only a short time, such as a few months. Others have to take it for a year or longer to feel better. That doesn't mean that one person is "sicker" or "tougher" than another. It just means that people are different and respond differently to medications. More and more young people are relying on Prozac for a growing number of reasons.

CHAPTER 3

Is Prozac Right for You?

*S*ometimes an antidepressant such as Prozac stops working. There are a few reasons why this may happen. A person's body may become "used" to the drug and build up a tolerance to it. Or the depression itself may become more severe because of situations in the person's life. In cases like these, some doctors decide that a supplementary medication is necessary. Because it has proved effective, doctors often give Prozac first to their patients and follow with another medication if Prozac does not help.

Shawna was taking Prozac for depression. After about three weeks on the drug, it was working. She felt less depressed and was interested in activities again. But after six

If you are under a great deal of stress and your depression becomes worse, you may try a supplementary medication.

months on Prozac, Shawna started to feel bad again. She didn't want to get out of bed, she didn't care about her schoolwork, and she didn't feel like hanging out with her friends. Shawna became angry and frustrated. She had thought her depression was over, but the symptoms had returned.

Shawna's father took her back to the doctor. The doctor increased Shawna's dosage of Prozac and gave her another antidepressant to try with it. He told Shawna to be patient and wait a few more weeks.

Shawna waited another four weeks, but she didn't feel any better. In fact, she felt worse. She still felt down, and sometimes she became nervous and jittery, or very angry.

34 | *She felt that she had to punch someone to make the anger go away. One morning, she got very angry because she missed the school bus. She threw one of her swimming trophies against the wall, and it broke. Shawna became afraid of her violent, angry feelings. Her father decided to take her to another doctor for help.*

Supplementary Medications

A supplementary medication may be another antidepressant that can "boost" the Prozac and help it work. It can also be a medicine from another family of antidepressants that may work better to relieve a person's depression.

One supplementary drug that is commonly used with Prozac is a stimulant called Ritalin, which regulates a person's behavior. It is usually given to children who have trouble concentrating. These children are sometimes depressed or have mood swings that include depression.

Doctors have found that, in combination, Ritalin often helps control the lack of concentration while Prozac combats the mood swings. The drug is becoming increasingly popular: More than 1.5 million children and teenagers are currently taking Ritalin.

"Mom, can I talk to you for a second?" Sam asked, walking into his mother's room.

"Sure, Sam. What's up?" his mother asked.

Sam sat down next to her on the bed. "I've been feeling kind of weird lately."

Sam's mother frowned. "What's wrong? Aren't you feeling well?" She felt Sam's forehead to see if he had a fever.

"It's nothing like that. I just feel sort of . . . I don't know—spaced out, I guess, and I can't concentrate at school. My teachers call on me to answer questions, and I don't even know what the question is. And I'm listening, I swear! I can't even pay attention to my favorite TV shows. Mom, I don't know what's going on. I've been feeling so sad and upset. I'm so frustrated!"

"I have noticed that you seem a little down. Don't worry, Sam," his mother said, hugging him. "I'm glad you came to me about this. Let's make an appointment with Dr. Ali. She can help us figure out what's going on."

Sam and his mother went to Dr. Ali, the family doctor. She listened while Sam explained his feelings and asked some questions about school, what was going on at home, and relationships with his friends. Then Dr. Ali smiled.

"It's going to be okay, Sam," she said. "I suggest that you make an appointment with

36 | *a therapist to talk about how you've been feeling. And I'm going to write you two prescriptions."*

"What are those for?" Sam asked, alarmed. "You said I wasn't sick!"

"You're just fine," Dr. Ali assured him. "The first medicine is an antidepressant, and it's for the down feelings you've been having. It's called Prozac. It will help you feel better. The second one is called Ritalin. It's for your concentration problem. It should help you feel more focused. I want you to take these exactly as prescribed, and we'll talk again in about a month. How does that sound?"

"Okay, I guess," Sam answered. He sounded unsure.

"It's going to be all right," Dr. Ali assured him. "We're going to help you."

Other supplementary drugs include Lithium, a mood-stabilizing drug, Valium, an antianxiety drug, and Zoloft, which is one of a few antidepressants that can be taken with Prozac.

Shawna's father took her to another doctor. The doctor asked her a lot of questions, and Shawna tried to explain the depression and the nervous, angry feelings. After talking, the doctor decided to have Shawna

It is very important that you tell your doctor exactly how you feel.

stop taking Prozac and the supplemental medication. He put her on another antidepressant, called Nardil. This medication is from another family of antidepressants.

One month later, Shawna met with the doctor again. She told the doctor she was not so depressed and wasn't nervous and angry all the time. At the doctor's suggestion, she was also meeting once a week with a therapist.

Speak Up

It may turn out that Prozac—or Prozac and a supplementary medication—is not right for you. Shawna's depression was not one that benefited from Prozac. It's very important to tell your doctor exactly

38 how you feel. Even a small detail about trouble sleeping or having no appetite can help the doctor decide whether Prozac is right for you or not. It can also help a doctor figure out whether therapy combined with medication may be beneficial.

You need to listen to your body very carefully if you are taking an antidepressant and it does not seem to be working the way it should. If you experience any of the following symptoms while taking Prozac, it is possible that your body is having a negative reaction to it:

- Severe mood swings (feeling very happy and then very angry or very sad)
- Violent feelings (wanting to hurt other people or things)
- Akathisia (extreme hyperactivity, which can include feeling tense or agitated, as well as a need always to move one's body—pacing, foot-tapping, squirming, or thrashing around while sleeping
- Paranoia
- Suicidal thoughts

If you experience any of these symptoms, you should call your doctor *immediately*.

The Problems and the Controversy

*W*hen *ten-year-old Timmy Becton of Lakeland, Florida, skipped school again in March 1996, the school sent a truant officer to his home to bring Timmy to school. But Timmy refused to go, and the truant officer left to get help. When the truant officer returned with a police officer, the boy was holding a shotgun, and he pointed it at the officers. There was a short stand-off between the police and the fourth-grader, and at one point Timmy used his three-year-old niece as a shield. The confrontation ended when Timmy's grandmother came home and took the gun away from him.*

Timmy was charged with armed kidnapping, aggravated assault, and criminal mischief. He had to spend one year in a juvenile

40 | *detention facility.*

Why did Timmy do these things? What made him act in such a violent way? His lawyer blames Prozac.

The criminal case against Timmy Becton is believed to be the first one involving a child's use of Prozac. Timmy had been taking Prozac for two months before his confrontation with the police. His doctor had prescribed the medication because he was hyperactive and was skipping school. His mother said that as the dosage was increased, Timmy would "get very mean and hateful for a couple of minutes [after taking it] and then he'd be back to himself again" (New York *Newsday*, 1996).

What happened to Timmy Becton? Some people—his lawyer and his parents—say that Prozac caused him to act in a destructive way.

Aggressive or Suicidal Behavior
Only three years after Prozac's introduction to the market, more than 20,000 reports of adverse reactions to the drug had been filed with the U.S. Food and Drug Administration (FDA). Adverse

reactions include any behavior that contradicts what the drug is supposed to do for a person. They could be violent mood swings, in which a person feels very happy and then suddenly very sad or angry; aggressive behavior, in which the person may act angry or violent; or thoughts of harming himself.

Timmy Becton is an example of such an adverse reaction to Prozac. The FDA has received countless reports of Prozac patients hurting or even killing others and then committing suicide. Many doctors believe these aggressive or suicidal tendencies existed in the person before he or she even started Prozac. But the number of negative reactions to this antidepressant is growing.

The use of antidepressants for children is increasing. In the past few years, prescriptions for Prozac and similar medications have reached more than 1.3 million annually. In the past three years, use of Prozac by children has grown three times faster than by adults. Children and teenagers are being given Prozac for a number of conditions, from shyness and eating disorders to anxiety and depression. Why are so many children and teenagers being given this antidepressant?

42

Fatima was taking Prozac for depression. Her doctor told her it would help, that her depression would lessen and she would feel like her old self again. "Many people have had great results with Prozac—you will, too," her doctor said.

Fatima waited for six weeks, but she didn't feel any less depressed. In fact, she had trouble falling asleep at night, and most of the time she felt jittery and nervous. She called her doctor and told her how she had been feeling. The doctor told her to be patient, that antidepressants take time to work. So Fatima waited for another month, but she still didn't feel any better. Sometimes she was very happy, but a few minutes later she became very sad or angry. One time she even knocked her little brother down because he went into her room without permission.

Fatima was scared. What was happening to her?

Many people have benefited from the use of Prozac. Millions have felt relief from depression, obsessive-compulsive disorder, and other conditions. But some doctors are prescribing this medication before exploring other possibilities, such as therapy or a change in diet and a regular exercise program.

It is debated whether or not Prozac is overprescribed.

The Problem of Overprescription

There are many reasons why doctors prescribe Prozac for children and adolescents without first looking for alternatives.

One of the reasons is that Prozac has been shown to work. However, although the effects of Prozac on adults have been researched, the drug has not been tested on children. Research with Prozac has not been conducted on children because of the possible legal risks if a problem occurs. Doctors rely on the positive effects that adults have experienced with the drug and hope that the same will occur with children and teenagers.

44

A Quick Fix

Some people fear that Prozac is being used by doctors who want to provide fast relief for predictable or bothersome problems. Patients are also attracted to the idea of fast relief and would rather take Prozac than be bothered with regular therapy visits. Family doctors and internists, not psychiatrists, are writing two-thirds of the prescriptions for antidepressants. Also, psychologists or therapists who cannot write prescriptions often work with family doctors who can provide medications. Psychiatrists, who are best qualified to decide if a patient needs an antidepressant, are writing only a small fraction of these prescriptions.

As a result, many children are not getting a full evaluation or complete psychological testing before starting medications like Prozac. This may be because parents are afraid that their children may be labeled "crazy." We already know that being depressed or needing an antidepressant does not mean you are crazy. But testing is necessary to ensure that Prozac, or another antidepressant, is in fact the best choice for you. Also, the dosages given to young people are often rough estimates, not based on factual information.

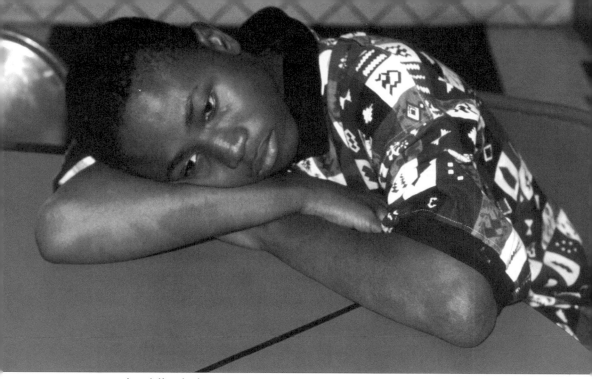
It can be difficult, but it is important to try to understand the nature of your depression.

Health-Care Costs

Sometimes a person's health insurance pays for most or all of the fees for doctors' appointments or X rays. It may also pay for therapy sessions. However, many insurance companies support the use of antidepressants rather than therapy because it costs them less money. It is cheaper for insurance companies to pay for a bottle of pills than for regular therapy appointments. Antidepressants like Prozac are sometimes prescribed to avoid high insurance costs.

Long-Term Effects

There is some concern about the long-term effects of antidepressants on the

45

46 | developing bodies of children and teen-
agers. About 9 million children have some
kind of emotional problem that makes it
hard for them to function. Last year,
doctors recommended or prescribed
Prozac and similar drugs 1.27 million
times for young people ages ten to nine-
teen. Were doctors aware of the possible
risk when they suggested Prozac?

Here is the controversy: Some doctors
and researchers believe that antidepressants
such as Prozac are perfectly fine for everyone and help them to handle their symptoms. Some even believe that Prozac can
"improve" a person beyond what he or she
was before the medication. They say that
millions of people have had very positive
results from Prozac and continue to do so.
And they are telling the truth. But are
these "new and improved" patients still the
same people while on Prozac, or have they
somehow been chemically changed?

Others believe that Prozac is a poison
and can only make a person's condition
worse. The opponents of Prozac think that
drugs are prescribed too quickly and easily,
and that although medications help the
symptoms of the depressed person, the
depression still exists beneath the surface.
Prozac may actually be smoothing over the

true problem or problems. What will
happen once the person is no longer on
Prozac?

*After his father died of cancer, Peter felt
down most of the time and was often very
nervous. He started to be afraid that he or his
mom would also die if they went outside. He
begged his mother not to leave the house or
leave him alone. Peter's mother became worried
and took her son to the family doctor. Peter
described his symptoms to the doctor, and she
wrote a prescription for Prozac.*

*About two weeks later, Peter started to feel
better. He was able to go to school and soc-
cer practice without feeling anxious. He also
noticed that he didn't feel depressed anymore.
Peter was relieved.*

*After almost a year on Prozac, Peter's
doctor suggested that he stop taking the antidepressant. She thought it was a good idea
to see if he could manage without it. Peter
agreed. He started to taper down his dosage
until he wasn't taking any Prozac.*

*At first, Peter didn't feel any different. But
that soon changed. One morning, he woke
up and felt as if a wave had hit him. He
couldn't stop thinking of his father, and he
was very depressed. Everything in his room
looked gray, and he felt as if a big, black
cloud surrounded him.*

48 *He tried to explain how he felt to his mother, but he was so sad and upset he couldn't speak. His mother called her friend Cindy, who was a social worker. She came over right away and had a talk with Peter. Cindy explained that although the Prozac may have helped Peter's symptoms of depression, he still had not talked about his father's death. Once the antidepressant completely left his system, the grief Peter that had pushed aside for the past year had come back to face him.*

Cindy offered to talk with Peter once a week. Peter wasn't sure. He said he often had so many feelings inside of him that he wouldn't know where to begin. But Cindy said he could talk about anything he wanted—or not talk at all. It would be his choice. Once a week, he would have a place to go where he could say whatever he wanted. He could get angry, be sad, or be happy. Most of all, he could be confident that whatever he and Cindy discussed would be confidential.

Peter decided he would meet with Cindy every Wednesday afternoon. He was nervous and a little scared, but he was hopeful.

Often, antidepressants like Prozac can help someone who is suffering from depression. But it cannot *cure* a person's depression. So what can a person do?

CHAPTER 5

The Right Way and the Wrong Way

*W*e have already discussed what can happen when Prozac is prescribed without first taking the necessary precautions and steps. But Prozac can be very effective, and the depressed person can benefit from it when it is used the right way. What is the "right way"?

The Right Way to Go

- **Keep in Touch:** Anyone who is taking an antidepressant should be monitored by a psychiatrist or licensed medical doctor. It is important to keep in touch with your doctor; call him regularly and let him know how you're feeling. You might even see him every few weeks or

Anyone who is taking an antidepressant should be monitored by a psychiatrist or licensed medical doctor.

once a month. That way, your doctor will know if the Prozac is working and can help you if you are not feeling the way you should.

- **Talk It Out:** It is very important that you have a therapist to talk to while taking Prozac. The two of you can work together as a team and talk about issues surrounding your depression. The benefit of combining an antidepressant with therapy is that they also work together as a team. While the antidepressant is working in your brain, helping to control your depression, you and your therapist can learn more about the source of your depression. Prozac can keep the

depression in check so you can help
yourself through therapy.

- **Find a Support Group:** There are
  people around you who are ready
  to help you through your situation.
  They could be your school counselor,
  teacher, minister or rabbi, or a few of
  your close friends. Some of your
  friends may even be in a similar situation and will understand what you are
  going through. Unfortunately, some
  people view persons on antidepressants or in therapy as "sick" or
  "crazy." This is false. The person in
  therapy or on medication is doing
  something positive to help him or
  herself. But even though you are doing
  the smart thing for *you*, it's important
  to be careful of whom you confide in
  about your depression or antidepressant. If you aren't sure whom you can
  talk to, your school nurse may be able
  to help you find a support network of
  students. You deserve to be able to
  share your feelings and frustrations
  with others who are experiencing
  some of the same things.
- **Write It Down:** Writing in a journal
  can help you keep track of and sort
  through your feelings on a day-to-

Writing in a journal can help you sort out your feelings.

day basis. You can find blank journals with or without lines (you can even draw pictures in your journal), and they are available in all sorts of colors and patterns. Find one that you like; keep it in one spot, and write in it at the same time every day. Many people like to write in a journal before going to sleep each night. Even if nothing really big happened that day, write down your thoughts, or things that may be bothering you. Write about your dreams. Your journal can be a special place where you can be yourself and talk about whatever you wish. | *53*

It has been six months since Audrey's doctor prescribed Prozac for her depression. Audrey has noticed that she feels less depressed. Her head feels clearer, and she doesn't turn to food anymore when she's down. She continues to visit her therapist weekly. Often she talks about how angry and sad she has felt since her parents' divorce. Audrey still has some bad days when she doesn't want to get up in the morning. But now she knows she is not alone. With a combination of therapy and Prozac, Audrey is on her way to beating her depression.

54 | Depression and other emotional conditions, such as OCD or anxiety, can be scary, lonely, and frustrating. No one should have to suffer through them. Luckily, however, help is available through therapy and medications. Prozac can be very helpful and effective, but it's important to be aware of the risks. Be smart: If your doctor thinks an antidepressant would be the best for you, talk to her about it. Don't be afraid to ask questions or express any doubts you may have. You and your doctor can come up with a solution that will make you both feel comfortable.

CHAPTER 6

You Can Help Yourself

*A*ntidepressants such as Prozac can help a person who is suffering through depression or some other emotional conditions. We have learned that Prozac is at its most effective when it is used correctly, with regular monitoring and awareness of the medication's side effects. Although research has shown some dangerous side effects, and negative situations have occurred with some patients, correct usage can help the person on Prozac obtain the best possible results.

Stopping Prozac
Over time, some patients will feel relief from their depression and stop taking Prozac. Others may decide, with their

Your doctor can outline a schedule for you to taper off your medication.

doctor, that Prozac is not working for them and another antidepressant may be a better choice. But how is this done? It's not as easy as it sounds—you can't just wake up one morning and stop Prozac "cold turkey." The important thing to remember is **not to stop taking any medication on your own**. Your body gets used to a medication that is taken for a long time and adjusts itself slightly to that drug. It is not good for your body to stop the drug abruptly. Your doctor will outline a schedule for you on tapering off your dosage. You will take a little less than your prescribed dosage on the first day and lower that amount every few days. This will continue until you aren't taking any Prozac.

While you are tapering off Prozac, and once you are completely off of it, you may experience a few mild withdrawal symptoms such as fatigue or a lack of energy. These will disappear as your body adjusts to the absence of Prozac.

Antidepressants like Prozac were created for people who suffer from depression and other emotional problems. They have been shown to be very helpful and have freed many people from painful, frustrating symptoms. Now you know the facts surrounding the controversy. Now you can make the right choices that will keep you happy and healthy.

Glossary

adolescence   The period of maturity between puberty and adulthood.

antidepressant   A drug that is used to relieve depression.

controversy   An issue that raises opposing views.

endorphin   Substance that exists naturally in the human body that can produce feelings of well-being.

hereditary   Passed down from one family member to another.

migraine   Condition involving severe headaches, often accompanied by nausea and vomiting.

obsessive-compulsive disorder (OCD) Psychological disorder marked by an irrational need to repeat certain behaviors.

phobia   An exaggerated fear of a specific object or situation.

premenstrual syndrome (PMS) Various physical and emotional symptoms that some women experience before menstrual periods.

supplementary medication   Medicine that is given in addition to or combined with a drug already being taken.

withdrawal   The period of time following the discontinuation of a drug; sometimes marked by uncomfortable physical and emotional symptoms.

Where to Go for Help

American Academy of Psychotherapists
   (AAP)
PO Box 607
Decatur, GA 30031
(404) 299-6336

American Counseling Association
5999 Stevenson Avenue
Alexandria, VA 22313
(703) 823-9800

Mental Health Information Center
National Mental Health Association
1021 Prince Street
Alexandria, VA 22314-2971
(800) 969-NMHA
http://www.nmha.org/

Prozac Survivors Support Group, Inc.
3080 Peach Avenue
Clovis, CA 93612
(209) 291-8661
http://www.dcn.davis.ca.us/%7EjonB/
   prosurv.html

Prozac Home Page
http://prozac.cwru.edu/

Suicide Prevention Hot Line
(800) 227-8922

In Canada
Canadian Mental Health Association
2610 Yonge Street
Toronto, ON M45 223
(416) 484-7750

For Further Reading

Ayer, Eleanor H. *Everything You Need to Know About Depression*. New York: Rosen Publishing Group, 1994.

Breggin, Dr. Peter R. and Ginger Ross. *Talking Back to Prozac*. New York: St. Martin's Press, 1995.

Breggin, Dr. Peter R. *Toxic Psychiatry*. New York: St. Martin's Press, 1991.

Clayton, Dr. Lawrence, and Carter, Sharon. *Coping with Depression*. New York: Rosen Publishing Group, 1992.

Gorman, Jack M., M.D. *The Essential Guide to Psychiatric Drugs*. New York: St. Martin's Press, 1990.

Graedon, Joe and Teresa, Ph.D. *The People's Guide to Deadly Drug Interactions*. New York: St. Martin's Press, 1995.

Larson, David E., ed. *Mayo Clinic Family Health Book*. New York: William Morrow and Company, Inc.

Simpson, Carolyn and Dwain. *Coping with Emotional Disorders*. New York: Rosen Publishing Group, 1991.

Wilkinson, Beth. *Drugs and Depression*. New York: Rosen Publishing Group, 1994.

Index

About the Author
Helen C. Packard is an editor and writer. She lives in New York City. This is her second Rosen book.

Photo Credits
Photo on p.43 by Seth Dinnerman; cover and all other photos by Ira Fox.